To Grandmother,

_____

With Love

_____

Nana,

Merry Christmas 1992. Thanks so much for coming down this Christmas. It was good to see you again. I hope to come and visit you sometime soon.

Love,
Andy

To Grandmother, With Love

Andrews and McMeel
A Universal Press Syndicate Company
Kansas City

ISBN: 0-8362-8001-6

Printed in Singapore
First U.S. edition

1   3   5   7   9   10   8   6   4   2

Edited by Linda Sunshine
Designed by Barbara Scott-Goodman
Produced by Smallwood and Stewart, Inc.
New York City

Introduction

$\mathcal{I}$ spent a lot of time with my grandmother, Nana Sunshine, when I was growing up and she helped me through a trying and often troubling adolescence. She was the one member of my immediate family who most understood me, or so I thought at the time. Looking back, I think it was not so much her understanding as it was the sheer force of her encouragement that helped me through those years.

My grandmother believed I was both smart and beautiful and, when I was with her, I sometimes believed it myself. She made me think I had good taste and common sense which, in her view, were the two most vital prerequisites for a woman of any age.

My relationship with my grandmother was not without its deep flaws—too often she sided with my mother, I thought. But she taught me many things about courage and independence—lessons which have served me well over the years.

I was fortunate to experience that special relationship that exists only between a child and a grandparent. Without the responsibility to discipline or punish, a grandparent wants only to love and be loved and gives freely to achieve both. No wonder then that it is often said that the best part of being a parent is in becoming a grandparent.

In words and pictures, this book celebrates the unique bond between a child and a grandmother. It is lovingly dedicated both to my Nana Sunshine and to all grandmothers who have been a guiding light and a source of inspiration to their grandchildren.

Linda Sunshine

It is as grandmothers that our mothers come
into the fullness of their grace,
when a man's mother holds his child
in her gladdened arms
he is aware of the roundness of life's cycle;
of the mystic harmony of life's ways.

Christopher Morley
Mince Pie

turned over on her face & stomach the morning she was 4 mos. old.
First smile ..... May 28th

NOTABLE EVENTS   DATES.

First Laugh _July 13th_

First Tooth _Aug 17th_ Second tooth _Aug 17th_

First Words _Button - chicken - (only unpronounceable)_

First Shoes _Oct - Brown - cloth tops - stiff soles_

First Short Clothes _Oct._

First Steps _Dec - 4th_

We never know
the love of the parent
till we become
parents ourselves.

Henry Ward Beecher

$\mathcal{T}$he other good idea was spending the summer with my grandmother Hy Dodd and her sister Glady Joe Cleary. Their relationship with me is different from that with the other grandchildren; we share secrets. And I probably talk to them a little more than my cousins or their own children do. I think they have a lot to say and I am more than willing to hear it. All of it. Whatever strikes them as important.

To me, they are important.

Whitney Otto
How to Make an American Quilt

Finally my grandmother came into the room. She had to lean across my bed to close the blinds. Her bosom was so close to my face. She smelled so nice. I pretended I was still sleeping and took the deepest breath of her I could. In that one moment, I think I knew what it was like to be loved. Really loved. I was so safe, so protected!

That's better than being pretty. I'll never forget it. The next thing I knew it was morning and I still didn't look like Audrey Hepburn. Now when I lie in bed with the blinds up and the moonlight spilling in, I'm not thinking I want to be somebody else, I just want my Nana back.

Terence McNally
Frankie and Johnny in the Claire de Lune

The closest friends
I have made all through life have been
people who also grew up close to a loved and
loving grandmother or grandfather.

Margaret Mead
Blackberry Winter

To Grandmother, With Love

It was a shock, even to her, how instantly and how deeply she loved her grandson. He was not quite two years old by then, a beautiful baby with a head that seemed adult in its shape—sharply defined, the golden hair trimmed close and neat. His firm, straight lips seemed adult as well, and he had an unchildlike way of walking. There was a bit of a slump in his posture, a little droop to his shoulders, nothing physically wrong but an air of resignation that was almost comical in someone so small. Pearl sat on the floor with him for hours, playing with his trucks and cars. "Vroom. Vroom. Roll it back to Granny, now." She was touched by his stillness.

Anne Tyler
Dinner at the Homesick Restaurant

*B*ells of the Past, whose long-forgotten music
Still fills the wide expanse,
Tingeing the sober twilight of the Present
With color of romance!

Bret Harte
The Angelus

So much of what is best in us is bound up in our love of family, that it remains the measure of our stability because it measures our sense of loyalty. All other pacts of love or fear derive from it and are modeled upon it.

Haniel Long
A Letter to St. Augustine

The past is a foreign country:
they do things differently there.

L.P. Hartley
The Go-Between

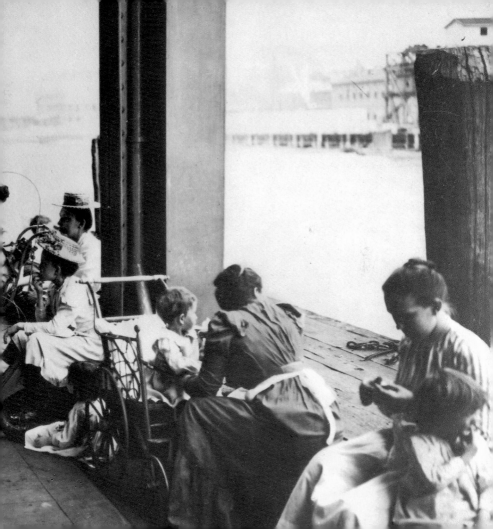

The personal legacy that our Grandmother Dianah Scarborough left behind is one of passionate pride and determination. Her erect carriage, penetrating gaze and strong sense of self made an indelible impression on all who met her. . . . She was a seamstress by trade, and professional pride kept her particularly interested in the immaculate appearance of her many offspring. After all, they were walking advertisements for her business. The ladies of Wilson—black and white— were well acquainted with her testy temperament, yet they continued to come to her because she could always be relied upon to deck them out in the latest dress and military style, often embellished with her own lace and special touches. She taught her three daughters dressmaking, needlepoint, and other homemaking skills—notably baking, canning, pickling and preserving—in which she excelled and expected excellence.

Norma Jean and Carole Darden
Spoonbread and Strawberry Wine

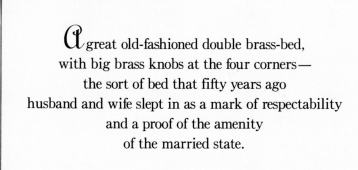

𝒜 great old-fashioned double brass-bed,
with big brass knobs at the four corners—
the sort of bed that fifty years ago
husband and wife slept in as a mark of respectability
and a proof of the amenity
of the married state.

Somerset Maugham

To Grandmother, With Love

Now that I've reached the age,
or maybe the stage,
where I need my children more
than they need me,
I really understand how grand it is
to be a grandmother.

Margaret Whitlam

To Grandmother, With Love

How confusing the beams from memory's lamp are;
One day a bachelor, the next a grampa.
What is the secret of the trick?
How did I get so old so quick?

Here lies my past. Goodbye I have kissed it;
Thank you kids. I wouldn't have missed it.

Ogden Nash

To Grandmother, With Love

She had been in the house, at different periods, as a child; in those days her grandmother lived there. Then there had been an absence of ten years, followed by a return to Albany before her father's death. Her grandmother, old Mrs. Archer, had exercised, chiefly within the limits of the family, a large hospitality in the early period, and the little girls often spent weeks under her roof—weeks of which Isabel had the happiest memory. The manner of life was different from that of her own home—larger, more plentiful, practically more festal; the discipline of the nursery was delightfully vague and the opportunity of listening to the conversation of one's elders (which with Isabel was a highly-valued pleasure) almost unbounded. There was a constant coming and going: her grandmother's sons and daughters and their children appeared to be in the enjoyment of standing invitations to arrive and remain, so that the house offered to a certain extent the appearance of a bustling provincial inn kept by a gentle old landlady who signed a great deal and never presented a bill. Isabel of course knew nothing about bills; but even as a child she thought her grandmother's home romantic. There was a covered piazza behind it, furnished with a swing which was a source of tremulous interest; and beyond this was a long garden, sloping down to the stable and containing peach-trees of barely credible familiarity. Isabel had stayed with her grandmother at various seasons, but some-how all her visits had a flavour of peaches.

Henry James
Portrait of a Lady

I do not believe in a child world. It is a fantasy world. I believe the child should be taught from the very first that the whole world is his world, that adult and child share one world, that all generations are needed.

Pearl Buck
To My Daughters, with Love

To Grandmother, With Love

We

should all have one person who knows

how to bless us despite the evidence,

Grandmother was that person to me . . .

Phyllis Theroux
California & Other States of Grace

Wilbur looked up. At the top of the doorway three small webs were being constructed. On each web, working busily was one of Charlotte's daughters . . .

It was a happy day for Wilbur. And many more happy, tranquil days followed.

As time went on, and the months and years came and went, he was never without friends . . . Charlotte's children and grandchildren and great grandchildren, year after year, lived in the doorway. Each spring there were new little spiders hatching out to take the place of the old . . .

Wilbur never forgot Charlotte. Although he loved her children and grandchildren dearly, none of the new spiders ever quite took her place in his heart. She was in a class by herself. It is not often that someone comes along who is a true friend and good writer. Charlotte was both.

E. B. White
Charlotte's Web

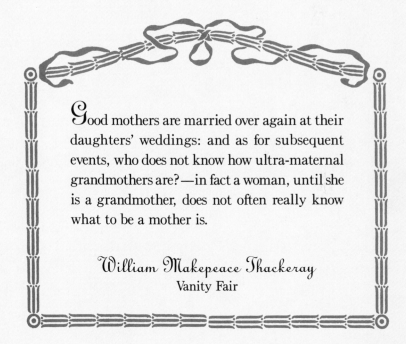

Good mothers are married over again at their daughters' weddings: and as for subsequent events, who does not know how ultra-maternal grandmothers are?—in fact a woman, until she is a grandmother, does not often really know what to be a mother is.

William Makepeace Thackeray
Vanity Fair

Over the river and through the woods,
To grandmother's house we go;
The horse knows the way
To carry the sleigh,
Through the white and drifted snow.

Lydia Maria Child
Flowers for Children

So many things we love are you,

I can't seem to explain except

by little things, but flowers

and beautiful handmade

things ~ small stitches.

So much of our reading and thinking,

so many sweet customs and so much

of our . . . well, religion. It is all *you*.

I hadn't realized it before.

This is so vague but do you see a little,

dear Grandma? I want to thank you.

Anne Morrow Lindbergh
Bring Me A Unicorn

$\mathcal{M}$ama and her mother were more I think opposites in many ways. But they had a connecting link: dreams. They were both dreamers. The difference was Mama's dreams solaced her; her mother's spurred her on. Mary Frances was a dreamer who did. She was a small, round, black-haired woman. She flew like a bee and sometimes like a bullet around her lanky, freckle-faced, slow-moving husband. And around her lanky, milk-skinned, dreaming daughter.

Jessamyn West
*The Second (or Perhaps Third)
Time Round*

She invoked the
understood silence
of the long married . . .

McCready Huston
The Platinum Yoke

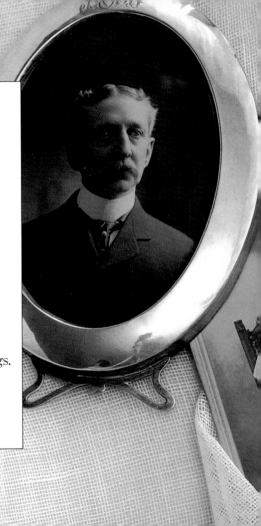

$\mathcal{E}$ach family,

however modest in its origin,

possesses its own particular

tale of the past—

a tale which can bewitch us

with as great a sense

of insistent romance

as can ever the traditions of kings.

Llewelyn Powys
Earth Memories

To Grandmother, With Love

I see it~
the past~
as an avenue lying behind;
a long ribbon of scenes, emotions.
There at the end of the avenue still,
are the garden and the nursery.

Virginia Woolf
A Sketch of the Past

The hours I spent with thee, dear heart,

Are as a string of pearls to me;

I count them over, every one apart,

My rosary, my rosary.

Robert Cameron Rogers
My Rosary

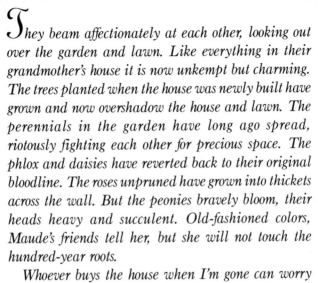

They beam affectionately at each other, looking out over the garden and lawn. Like everything in their grandmother's house it is now unkempt but charming. The trees planted when the house was newly built have grown and now overshadow the house and lawn. The perennials in the garden have long ago spread, riotously fighting each other for precious space. The phlox and daisies have reverted back to their original bloodline. The roses unpruned have grown into thickets across the wall. But the peonies bravely bloom, their heads heavy and succulent. Old-fashioned colors, Maude's friends tell her, but she will not touch the hundred-year roots.

Whoever buys the house when I'm gone can worry about that. I won't separate the peony roots. She brings blooms into the house filling the vases. Even as she and Hal talk, the heavy flowers shed slowly and quietly over the magazines and books that sprawl across the library table.

A. C. Hoffmann
Happy Families

for your grandmama

𝐼 will wait for her in the yard that Maggie and I
made so clean and wavy yesterday afternoon. A
yard like this is more comfortable than most
people know. It is not just a yard. It is like an
extended living room.

Alice Walker
Everyday Use

A child of our grandmother Eve,
a female;
or, for thy more sweet understanding,
a woman.

William Shakespeare
Love's Labour's Lost

$\mathcal{T}$here was real beauty to the old idea of living and dying where you were born. You could hold a place in a kind of eternity. Your grandparents took you out to dinner Sunday nights at the country club, and you could take your own grandchildren there when that time came: more little tow-heads, as squint-eyed and bony-legged and Scotch-Irish as hillbillies. And those grandchildren, like figures in a reel endlessly unreeling, would partake of the same timeless, hushed, muffled sensations.

Annie Dillard
An American Childhood

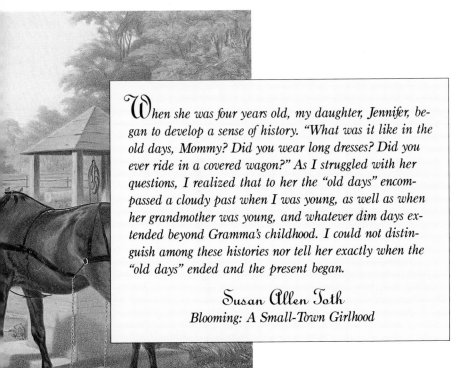

When she was four years old, my daughter, Jennifer, began to develop a sense of history. "What was it like in the old days, Mommy? Did you wear long dresses? Did you ever ride in a covered wagon?" As I struggled with her questions, I realized that to her the "old days" encompassed a cloudy past when I was young, as well as when her grandmother was young, and whatever dim days extended beyond Gramma's childhood. I could not distinguish among these histories nor tell her exactly when the "old days" ended and the present began.

Susan Allen Toth
Blooming: A Small-Town Girlhood

$\mathcal{A}$urora looked her [daughter] over thoughtfully. "Yes, you have a good deal more of your grandmother's nature than you have of mine," she said. "She was a great advocate of half measures too."

Larry McMurtry
Terms of Endearment

My mother has stopped talking. She raises her eyebrows, asking me to respond to her. Soon I know if I hold silence she will take a deep breath and straighten her shoulders. "Daughter," she will say, in a voice that is stern and admonishing, "always a woman must be stronger than the most terrible circumstance. You know what my mother used to say? Through us, the women of the world, only through us can everything survive."

An image comes to me. I see generations of women bearing a flame. It is hidden, buried deep within, yet they are handing it down from one to another, burning. It is a gift of fire, transported from a world far off and far away, but never extinguished. And now, in this very moment, my mother imparts the care of it to me. I must keep it alive, I must manage not to be consumed by it, I must hand it on when the time comes to my daughter.

Kim Chernin
In My Mother's House

When I have a little girl
all the rules will be different
And I will never say to her,
"When you are a mother
you will understand
why all these rules
are necessary."
My mother says . . .
her mother used to say it too.

Charlotte Zolotow
When I Have a Little Girl

My grandmothers were strong.
They followed plows and bent to toil,
They moved through fields sowing seed.
They touched earth and grain grew.

Margaret Abigail Walker
Lineage

*I*n Africa age is equated with wisdom, since the original culture was the accumulated knowledge and skills which come only with experience and time. Old people were respected and honoured. Young people listened to them, and their advice was sought to solve quarrels and to pass judgement in all aspects of village life. Having gone through many seasons and listened to their fathers and grandfathers, they could foresee patterns in the rains and recognize early signs of drought. They knew the secrets of the animals and of the plants, the traditional herbal remedies, and the rituals to keep gods happy or to prevent their wrath. The elders were the library in which was stored all the knowledge the tribe needed to survive and to thrive. As in the herds of elephant, where it is the old matriarchs who lead the younger animals to the waterholes and the feeding grounds, the old people steered the village on to the right path.

Kuki Gallman
I Dreamed of Africa

My mother's hair was a color you could feel more than see—a very, very black, as black and shiny as water at the very bottom of a deep well. And winding through her bun were two white hairs, like little ripples when tiny stones are thrown in the water. . . . She always found a reason why I should learn. She told me once she had wanted to be a schoolteacher, just like the missionaries who had taught her . . . she sang me a little song—about a little mouse who stole lamp oil. Do you remember? I used to sing you that song.

Amy Tan
The Kitchen God's Wife

To Grandmother, With Love

Hilary went to the Venetian mirror, set the flowers on the table under it, then walked back to stand at the fireplace and observe the effect. There in the mirror across the room she caught a glimpse of herself as Sargent had captured her, in the drawing over the mantel, at twenty five. There stood Age with Youth, like a ghost, suspended over her head. Without her glasses, Hilary saw the two figures slightly blurred, as if seen through water. . . , they seemed strangely alike, as perhaps they were; one does not become less oneself with the years, but more so; that self-intoxicated, quizzical young charmer was less than the Hilary confronting her with just the same slightly mocking lift of her chin.

She was not really seeing with her eyes. As always in this room, she was borne away on half-conscious stretches of memory. What "they" never understood about her solitary life was that it was a solitude so inhabited by the past, that she was never alone in it. . . .

May Sarton
Mrs. Stevens Hears the Mermaid Singing

I must study politics and war that my sons may have liberty to study mathematics and philosophy. My sons ought to study mathematics and philosophy, geography, natural history, naval architecture, navigation, commerce, and agriculture, in order to give their children a right to study painting, poetry, music, architecture, statuary, tapestry, and porcelain.

John Adams
Letter to Abigail Adams
May 12, 1780

It
is worthwhile for
anyone to have
behind him a few
generations of
honest, hard-working
ancestry.

*John Phillips
Marquand*
The Late George Apley

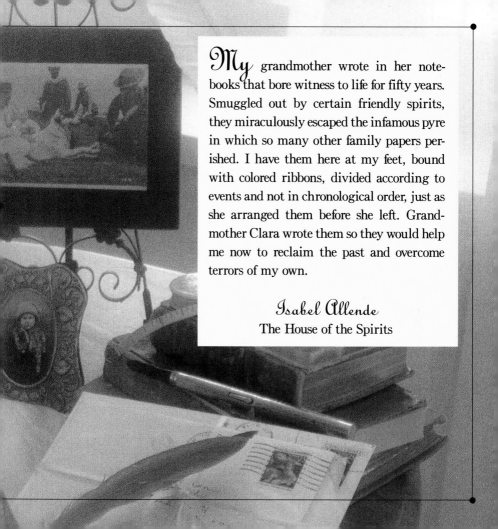

My grandmother wrote in her note-books that bore witness to life for fifty years. Smuggled out by certain friendly spirits, they miraculously escaped the infamous pyre in which so many other family papers per-ished. I have them here at my feet, bound with colored ribbons, divided according to events and not in chronological order, just as she arranged them before she left. Grand-mother Clara wrote them so they would help me now to reclaim the past and overcome terrors of my own.

Isabel Allende
The House of the Spirits

There is even room enough
For the letters of my mother's mother,
Elizabeth,
That have been pressed so long
Into a corner of the roof
That they are brown and soft,
And liable to melt as snow.

Hart Crane
My Grandmother's Love Letters

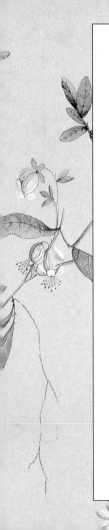

$\mathcal{G}$randmother's mother: her age, I guess,
Thirteen summers, or something less;
Girlish bust, but womanly air;
Smooth, square forehead with uprolled hair;
Lips that lover never kissed;
Taper fingers and slender wrist;
Hanging sleeves of stiff brocade;
So they painted the little maid.

O Damsel Dorothy! Dorothy Q.!
Strange is the gift that I owe to you;
Such a gift as never a king
Save to daughter or son might bring, —
All my tenure of heart and hand,
All my title to house and land;
Mother and sister and child and wife
And joy and sorrow and death and life!

O lady and lover, how faint and far
Your images hover, — and here we are,
Solid and stirring in flesh and bone, —
Edward's and Dorothy's — all their own, —
So you shall smile on us brave and bright
As first you greeted the morning's light,
And live untroubled by woes and fears
Through a second youth of a hundred years.

Oliver Wendell Holmes
Dorothy Q., A Family Portrait

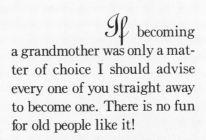

If becoming a grandmother was only a matter of choice I should advise every one of you straight away to become one. There is no fun for old people like it!

Hannah Whitall Smith
Philadelphia Quaker

When I was growing up, the family would have described themselves as close. They saw each other on Sundays and in between called on the phone. They all lived within about a twenty-five mile radius and when they said "The Family" we all knew what they meant. They didn't go in for elaborate explanations but instead seemed to operate by subtle signaling like flocks of birds.

Nancy Potter
Light Timber

Acknowledgements

Excerpt reprinted by permission of Random House, Inc., from *How to Make an American Quilt* by Whitney Otto. Copyright © 1991 by Whitney Otto.

The excerpt from *Frankie and Johnny in the Clair de Lune* included in this volume is reprinted by permission of the author and Dramatist's Play Service, Inc. The stock and amateur performance rights in the play are controlled exclusively by Dramatist's Play Service, Inc., 440 Park Avenue South, New York, NY 10016. No stock or amateur performance of the play may be given without obtaining in advance the written permission of the Dramatist's Play Service Inc., and paying requisite fee. All inquiries concerning rights (other than stock and amateur rights) should be addressed to Gilbert Parker, % William Morris Agency Inc., 1350 Avenue of the Americas, New York, NY 10019. Copyright © 1988 by Terence McNally.

Excerpt reprinted by permission of Random House Inc. from *Dinner at the Homesick Restaurant* by Anne Tyler. Copyright © 1989 by Anne Tyler.

Excerpt reprinted by permission of Doubleday, a division of Bantam Doubleday Dell Publishing Group, Inc. from *Spoonbread and Strawberry Wine* by Norma Jean & Carole Darden. Copyright © 1978 by Norma Jean & Carole Darden.

Excerpt reprinted by permission of HarperCollins Publishers from *Charlotte's Web* by E.B. White. Copyright © 1952 by E.B. White. Text copyright renewed © 1980 by E.B. White.

Excerpt reprinted by permission of Harcourt Brace Jovanovich, Inc. from "The Second (or Perhaps Third) Time Round" by Jessamyn West in *The Collected Stories by Jessamyn West*. Copyright © 1986 by Jessamyn West.

Excerpt reprinted by permission of HarperCollins Publishers from *An American Childhood* by Annie Dillard. Copyright © 1987 by Annie Dillard.

Excerpt reprinted by permission of Little, Brown and Company from *Blooming: A Small-Town Girlhood* by Susan Allen Toth. Copyright © 1978, 1981 by Susan Allen Toth.

Excerpt reprinted by permission of Tickner & Fields, a Houghton Mifflin Company imprint, from "In My Mother's House: A Daughter's Story" by Kim Chernin. Copyright © 1983 by Kim Chernin. All rights reserved.

Excerpt reprinted by permission of HarperCollins Publishers from "When I